This Walker book belongs to:

CHEERY STREET
CHEERY GARDEN

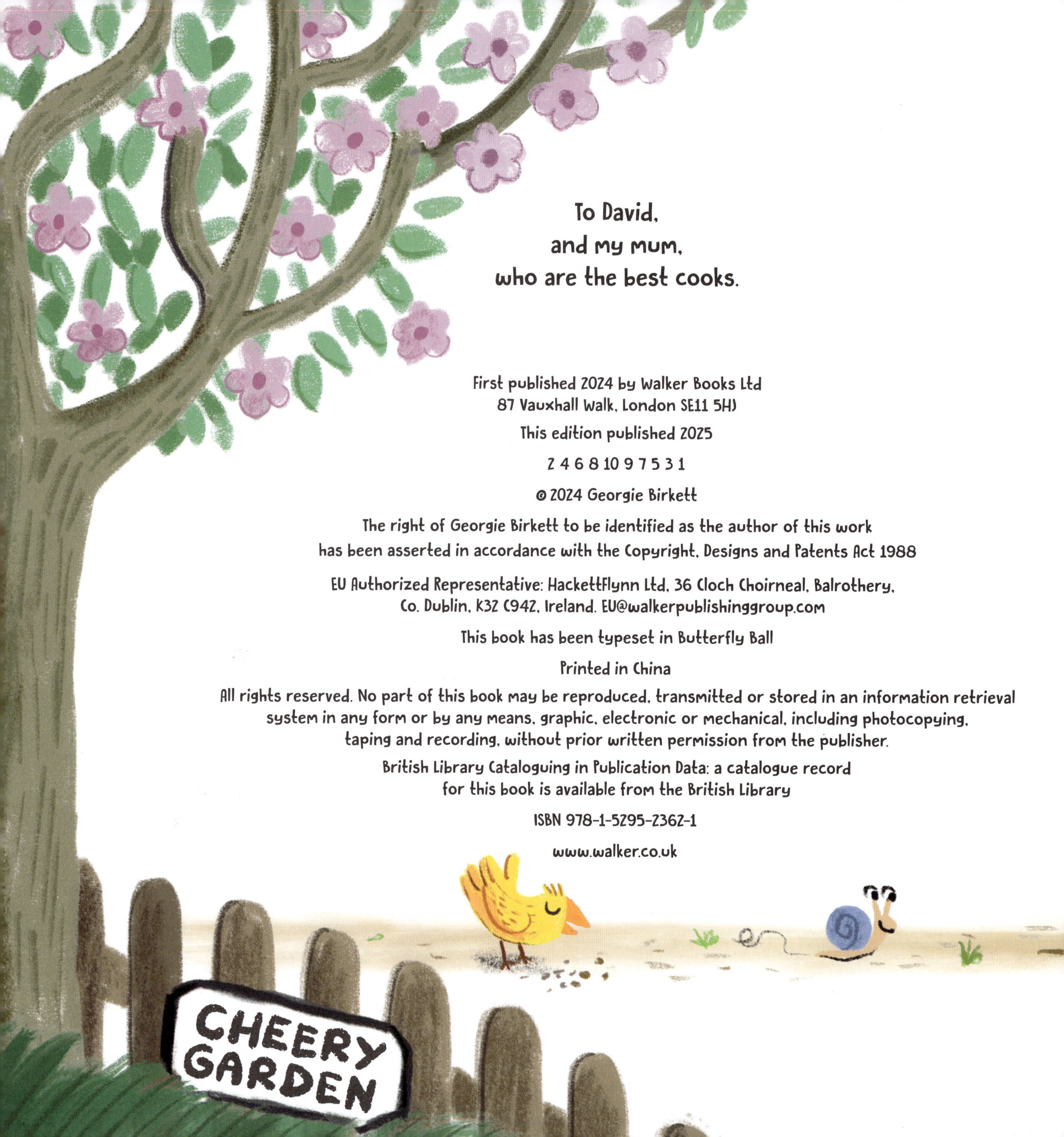

To David,
and my mum,
who are the best cooks.

First published 2024 by Walker Books Ltd
87 Vauxhall Walk, London SE11 5HJ

This edition published 2025

2 4 6 8 10 9 7 5 3 1

EU Authorized Representative: HackettFlynn Ltd, 36 Cloch Choirneal, Balrothery, Co. Dublin, K32 C942, Ireland. EU@walkerpublishinggroup.com

This book has been typeset in Butterfly Ball

Printed in China

British Library Cataloguing in Publication Data: a catalogue record for this book is available from the British Library

ISBN 978-1-5295-2362-1

www.walker.co.uk

SNACK, PLEASE!

by Georgie Birkett

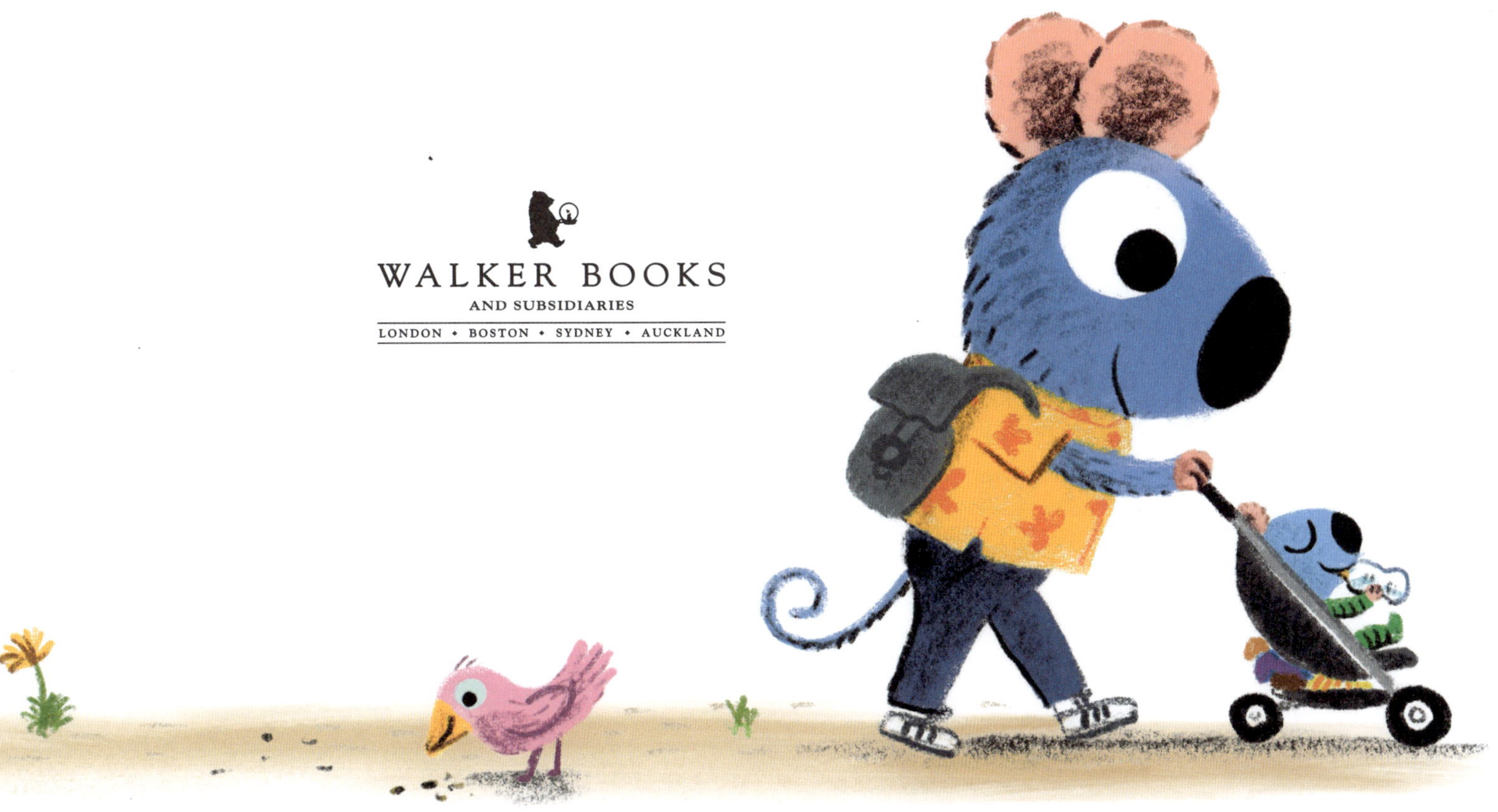

WALKER BOOKS
AND SUBSIDIARIES
LONDON • BOSTON • SYDNEY • AUCKLAND

When she was a baby, Gertie LOVED food. She would eat mashed-up veg, mushed-up fruit ...

smooshed-up anything really.

Sometimes even dusty old crackers from the *very* bottom of the nappy bag.

Gertie's daddy absolutely loved making food for her, and baby Gertie would gobble up all of his yummy meals.

As Gertie got older, she would still eat most things. She also ate … *other* things. Like grass, mud, daisies, and once she *even* ate a slug! (Yuck!)

Gertie nibbled at noses and chewed on Grandma's glasses.

She would try eating *anything*.

But then Gertie discovered something new. Something she loved to eat more than anything else...

CHEERY PARK
SNA

CKS!

Gertie had lots of favourite snacks.
(Do you, too?) Gertie loved:

Sweet
banana chips!

Carroty
rice cakes!

Crunchy munchy crackers!

And toast in bed.

But, with all this snacking ...

Gertie was always too full up to eat her meals!

Daddy loved to make all kinds of tasty food ...

but Gertie
just wanted
(you guessed it) ...

SNACKS!

When Daddy picked Gertie up
from school, he would say,
"Did you have a good day?"
And Gertie would say:
SNACK, PLEASE!
3
4
2
5
1

In fact, no matter what they did together, Gertie would say:

Daddy, it has to be said, was feeling snacked-out.

So, he decided to take Gertie to visit Grandma at the community garden, where everyone was helping pick fruit and veg.

And can you believe it?
Gertie only asked for a snack ONCE!
She was simply too busy getting
her hands mucky.

"Look at all this delicious food," said Grandma.
"And you picked it by yourself!
What would you like to do with it, Gertie?"

"Maybe," said Gertie, feeling a bit shy, "we can take it home and make a special dinner together, Daddy? For all my friends?"

"Gertie, are you saying ... dinner, please?" said Daddy. He could hardly believe it!

Back at home, Gertie and Daddy chopped and mixed, stirred and grated, to make the most delicious meal.

And while dinner was cooking ...

Gertie got the table ready for her friends.

When Daddy pulled dinner out of the oven, Gertie shouted,

She was so proud, in fact ...

she ate EVERYTHING on her plate, until her food was ALL gone.

"You know, Daddy, I think I might be too full for snacks!" she said.

peeta
Charlie

Gertie still eats some snacks, of course.
Everyone does, don't they?
But she also eats a lot more dinners.

Carroty Mash Monday

MASH MASH

Sushi Saturday

CHOP CHOP

And then she discovered something wonderful, something she loved to eat more than anything else...

"PUDDING, PLEASE!"

CHEERY STREET
CHEERY GARDEN

Welcome to

Cheery Street

Here on Cheery Street, you'll find happy stories about busy kids and even busier (and a little tired!) parents – full of playtime, snack time and cosy bedtimes.

Have you got these ones?

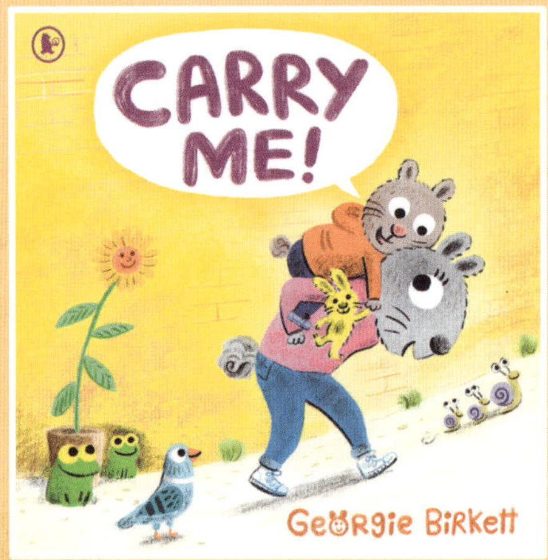

978-1-5295-1660-9

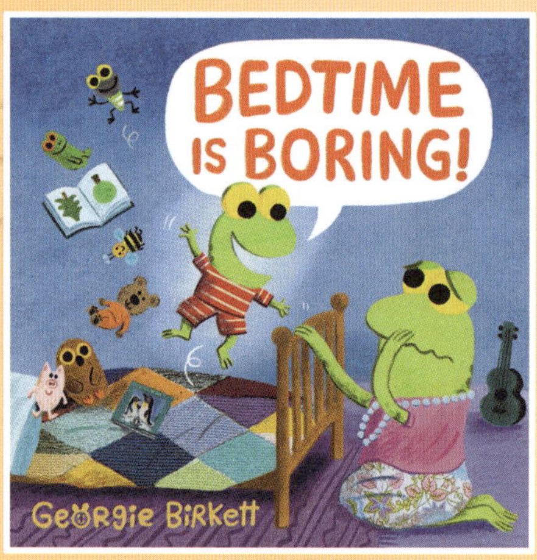

978-1-5295-2077-4

About these books, Georgie Birkett says:

"Parenting is a journey of joy, tears and tantrums. It is wonderful to share these experiences in the warm and friendly setting that is Cheery Street, a place where children and caregivers can explore life's challenges together, with plenty of laughs and hugs along the way!"